7/93

FILTER PEOPLE

Understanding and Confronting Our Prejudices

JIM COLE

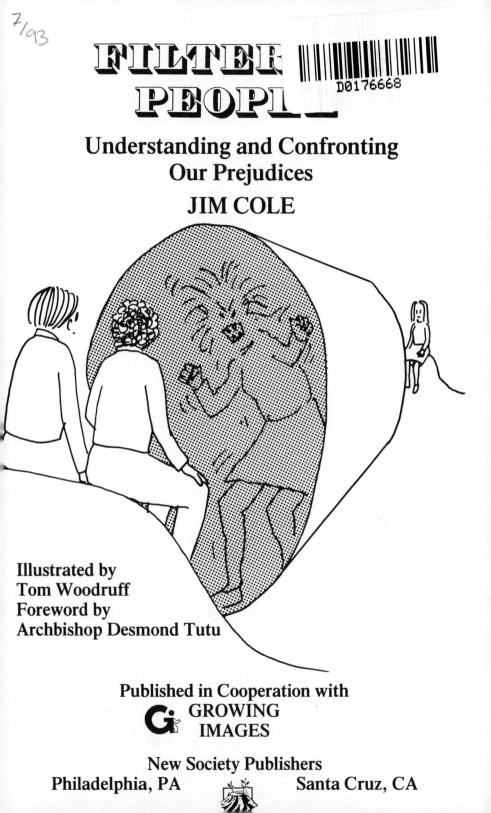

Illustrated by
Tom Woodruff
Foreword by
Archbishop Desmond Tutu

Published in Cooperation with
G GROWING
IMAGES

New Society Publishers
Philadelphia, PA   Santa Cruz, CA

This edition is a cooperative effort between Growing Images and New Society Publishers. A non-trade edition was self-published by Growing Images in 1987.

Inquiries regarding requests to reprint all or part of *Filtering People: Understanding and Confronting Our Prejudices* should be addressed to:
New Society Publishers
4527 Springfield Avenue
Philadelphia, PA 19143 USA

ISBN 0-86571-176-3 Paperback
ISBN 0-86571-175-5 Hardcover

Printed in the United States of America on partially recycled paper by Wickersham Printing, Lancaster, PA.

Illustrated by Tom Woodruff.

For more information about Growing Images: "Picture books of the Human Experience" please contact:
Jim Cole
627 Kay Street
Fairbanks, Alaska 99707 USA

New Society Publishers is a project of the New Society Educational Foundation, a nonprofit, tax-exempt, public foundation. Opinions expressed in this book do not necessarily represent positions of the New Society Educational Foundation.

Dedication

To my sons, Joe and Doug: May those who affect your lives never make judgments about you without first experiencing the good in you that I know.

Foreword

In Africa we have a saying that a person is a person through other people. Our humanity stems from our ability to relate to other people and to God. When we alienate ourselves from each other we debase ourselves. What self-inflicted poverty!

It seems we have great difficulty in accepting each other, perhaps because we cannot accept ourselves. Too often we are looking over our shoulders checking, "Am I alright?" Comparing ourselves against others; yet we are not like anybody else. No two people are the same. That is quite mind-boggling and what a miracle of God. He has made each person different that each may be valued for that very difference, reflecting God's love and the diversity of creation. A creation of which we are all a part not just as equals but more than that, as family, the human family, God's family.

You do not choose your family; they are God's gift to you as you are to them. You may not always agree with your bother or your sister but you can never renounce them. They are always your family. If we were to see each person as a brother or a sister how could we ever let anyone go hungry, or cold, or lonely, or fight wars against them, or be treated differently to ourselves? No, you would want the very best for your family. It is when we have this attitude that we become most fully human and, strangely, we no longer need to look over our shoulder.

Desmond M. Tutu,
The Anglican Archbishop of Cape Town, South Africa

Introduction

Increasingly on college campuses and in public schools just like in the rest of society, reports are surfacing of cultural, racial, and ethnic conflicts that are reminiscent of pre-1960 attitudes. Jim Cole and I are both psychologists who are concerned about these social issues and about what people do to each other, our planet, and as a result to our children's future. In Jim's book *Filtering People*, he and illustrator Tom Woodruff graphically cut to the heart of racism, ageism and sexism. The possibility of peace depends on inclusion, acceptance, and the realization that strength comes through the richness of difference more than through purification.

Desmond Tutu, who knows well of Jim's work, requested two hundred copies of this book to use in the struggles of South Africa. I understand Tutu's choice because I find *Filtering People* particularly useable in educational settings with diverse populations. I also feel it is a potent book in religious settings where many of the beliefs about the singularity of access to God aggravate and underscore difference rather than unification.

In this book, Dr. Cole speaks to one of the major "monsters" that we must face in our time if we are to move through the friction and disparity of difference to the strength that lies on the other side. What we know psychologically is that if we turn and face what scares us the most, not only will we become more of who we are, but we will transform what has so frightened us. I would call this book a road map to help individuals make that journey.

Dr. David McMurry
Educator and Psychologist
Creator of "Finding Meaning on an Endangered Planet"
Bayside, California

Sometimes I don't receive what I want

while someone else is getting it,

and I feel hurt

and angry.

I wonder if it's because of the way I am.

3

So I attack the other person.

I can see that the other person
is different from me

in ways that I can't change.

So I try to show that I'm more deserving than that other person so that I can get what I need

and won't doubt myself.

Some people look different from
me in ways that I can easily
see,

and I continue to doubt myself
and feel fearful.

Later on I hear people talking
that I can't understand

and I feel left out and somehow
threatened.

Sometimes I see people who look
very much like me.

Yet they seem to see a very different
meaning in the world than I do

and I find this
uncomfortable.

I want to know that I am all right,

so I ask someone close to me.

We start to question ourselves,

and it is very uncomfortable.

We then conclude that "we are
all right".

19

Since we are all right and they aren't like us, then...

. . . We're sure glad we're not like them!

So we build a filter that brings
us together

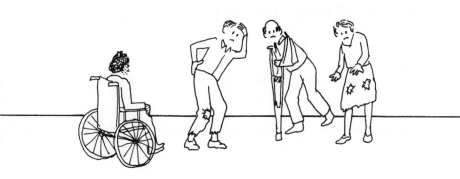

and lets us see them, while
protecting us from questioning
ourselves.

With the filter in place our self-doubts seem to disappear,

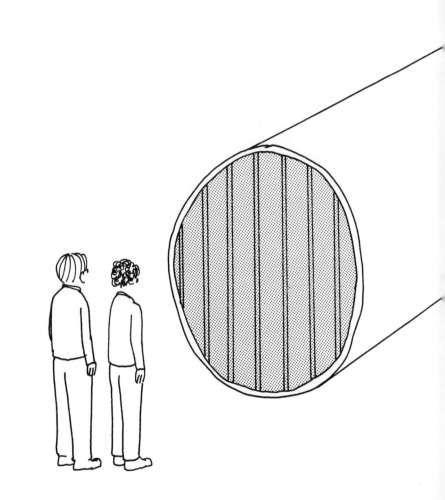

and we see others as all wrong.

Now we feel *brave* and *strong* and able to watch people who appear frightening to us.

In fact the worse they look the better we feel because we are different.

I don't understand them and won't risk showing myself.

So I build a bigger filter and talk about *them*.

THEY ARE NOTHING BUT...

THEY ALWAYS WANT...

THEIR TYPE NEVER...

29

The bigger filter seems to predict
what they are going to do,

and this comforts me.

So that I can feel safer,

I give them all one name....

a name I wouldn't call myself.

The name I give them doesn't
describe what they are doing

but limits them and implies that they are unchanging.

Once I have named them, I feel
safer

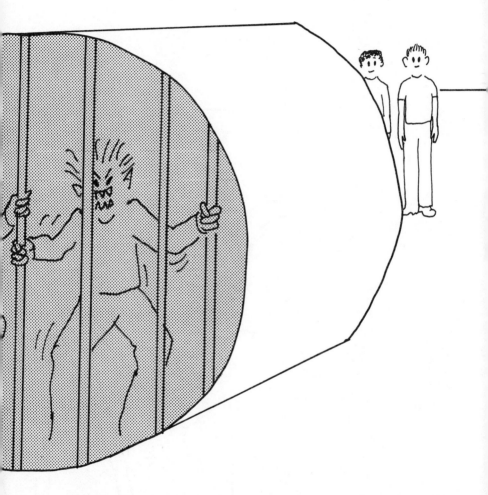

because I know they are not like me.

I don't feel a need to treat them like I want to be treated

because *they* are different.

Since they are _so_ different from us

they become more interesting to us

and even more frightening!!

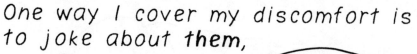

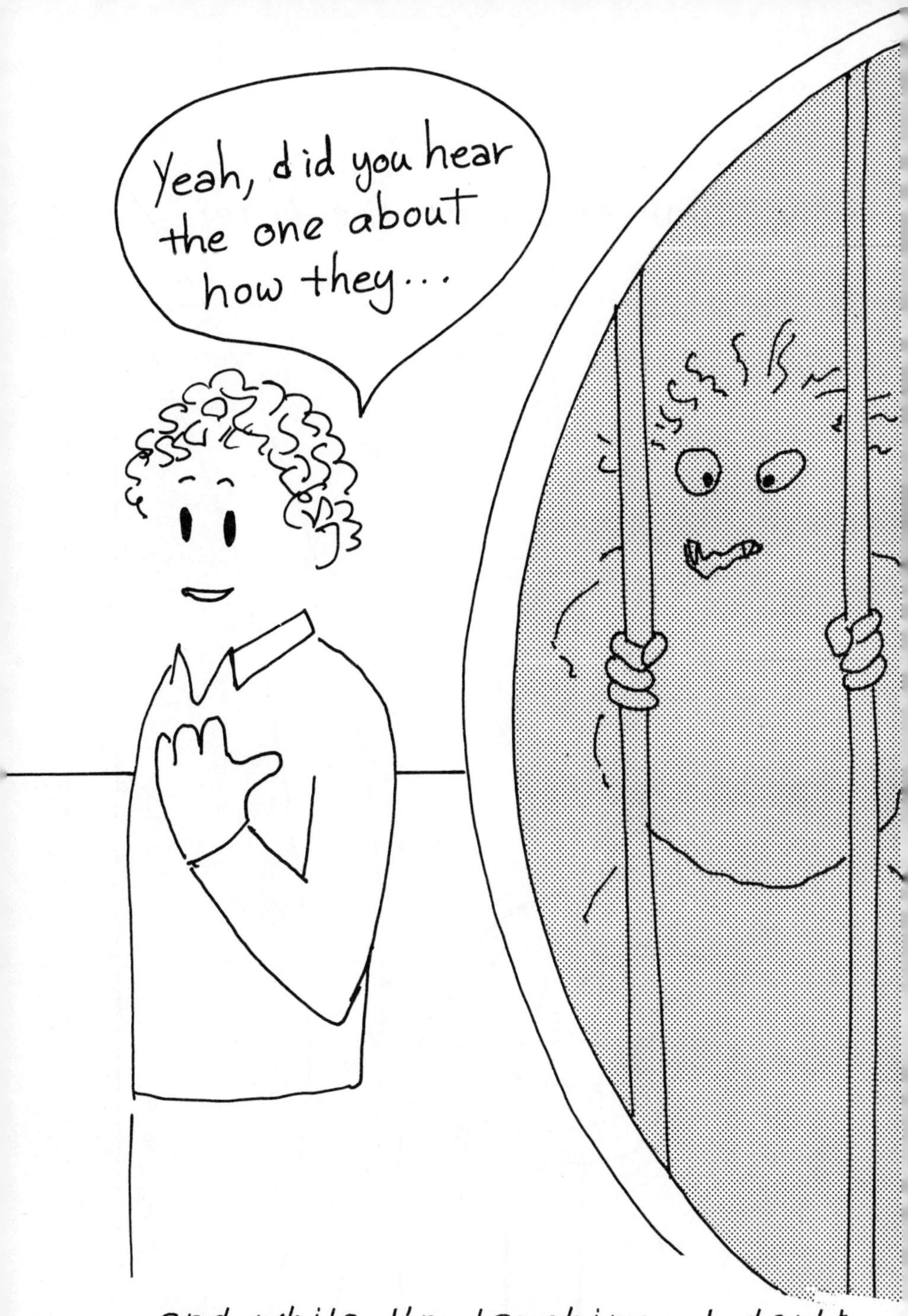

and while I'm laughing, I don't need to understand **them.**

My laughter builds the filter stronger

for my protection!!

Sometimes I get to know one of them
and we get close.

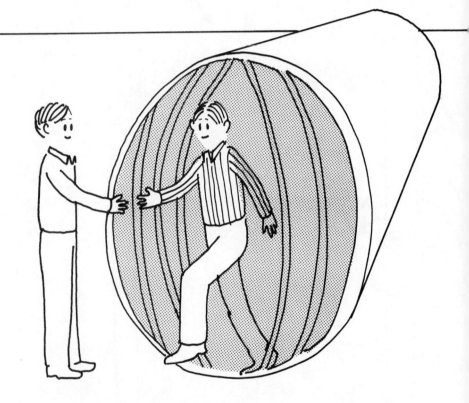

I see that maybe my filter is wrong
and we are alike in our needs,

then suddenly I catch myself

and **fix** my filter.

47

When I've been close to someone for
a long time

and I become angry with that person,

I simply roll my filter between us.

While the filter gives me strength in my position,

it also leaves me feeling alone and separate from this person.

So I find someone who agrees with me and have

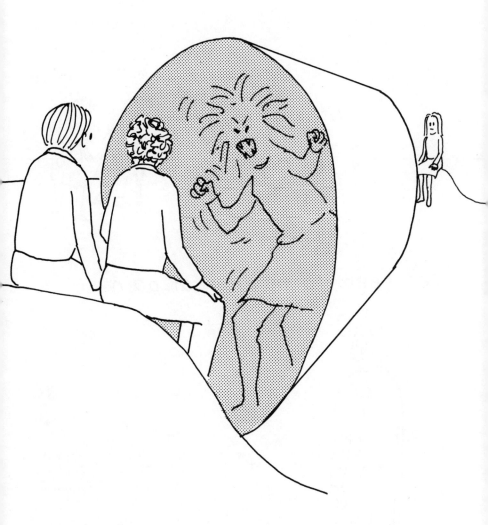

him look through my filter with me.

Sometimes I see people who look like me

yet seem to be in real pain.

Their pain is uncomfortable for me.

53

So I use my filter

and see them differently.

When I have a problem,

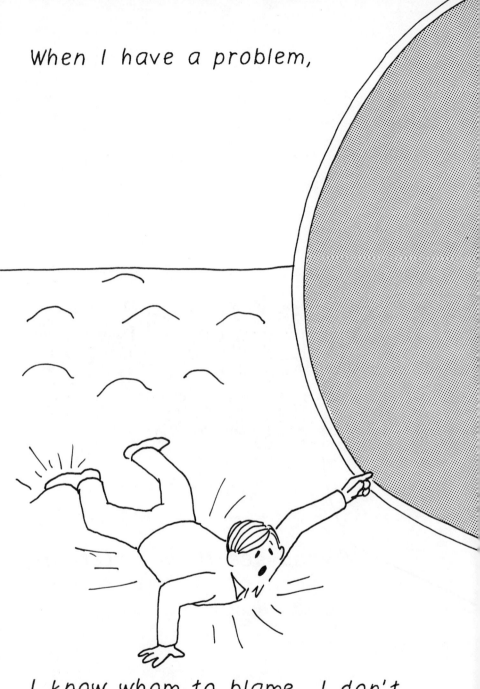

I know whom to blame. I don't
know how they did it,

but it's just like them.

When it seems to others that a situation is unclear,

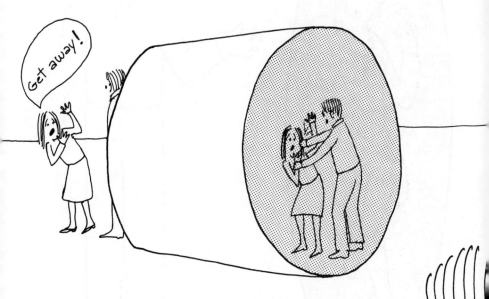

my filter clears it up...

one way or another.

61

My filter is so powerful that it can cut right through rumors with only one clue.

The filter saves time and effort while it provides

a feeling of dependability.

When I don't know whom to point my filter toward,

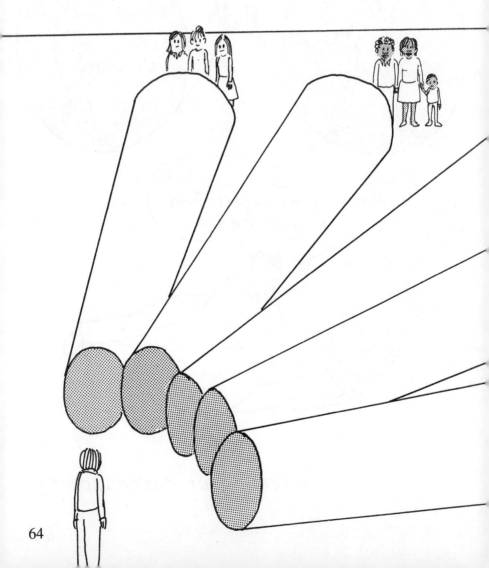

I find those who look or sound different from me.

The filter is very powerful. Using only a few outward clues...

my filter seems to detect their inner needs and values.

It's a real problem to trust one of them.
They don't value life like we do.
If you give them an inch...
Actually, They're more like animals.

My filter seems to work best at greater distances

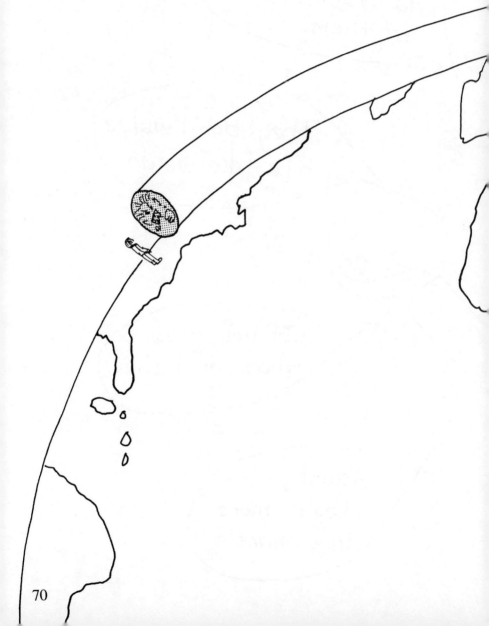

where I don't have **them** or **their**
interference around.

Sometimes my filter screens out everyone,

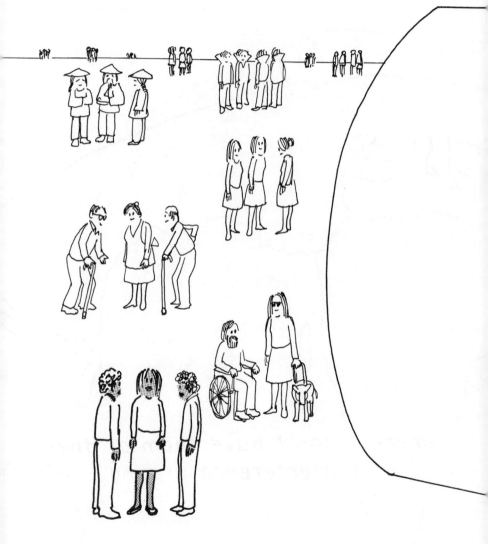

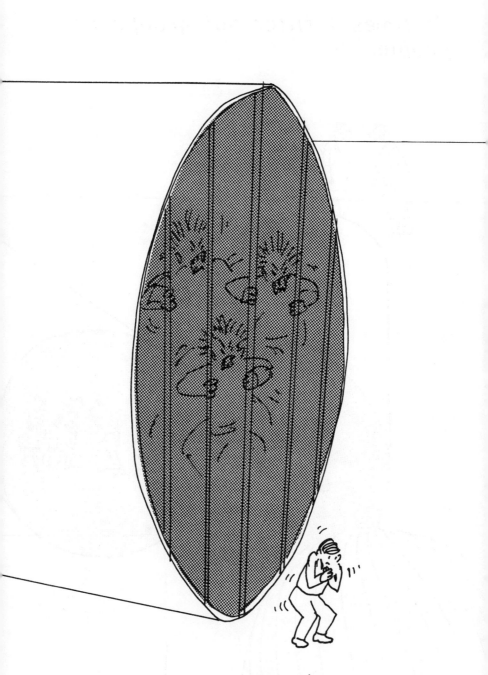

and I'm all alone.

At times I filter out groups of people

as being less valuable.

Then I discover I've become one of them and filtered myself,

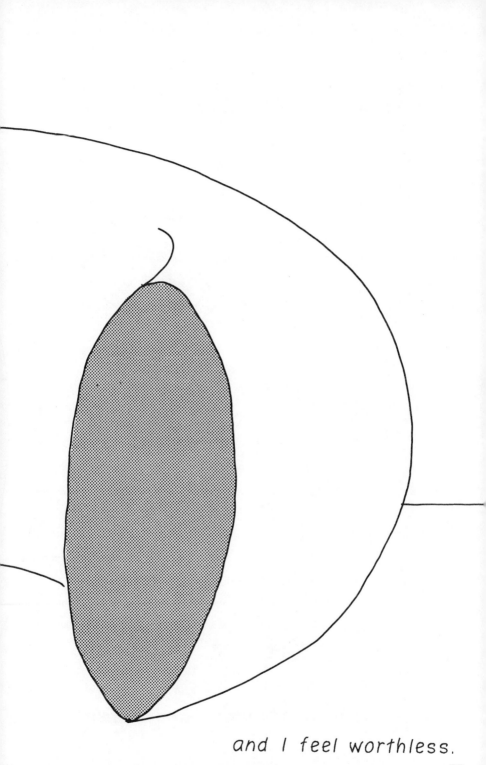

and I feel worthless.

Sometimes when I'm feeling worthless and not very good about who I am,

At least I'm not one of them.

I just build a stronger and safer filter.

Whenever I hear that **one of them**
has done something terrible,

I use that information to keep my filter strong

for _all_ of them!!

When one of us occasionally does
something that hurts some of them...

it's understandable.

At times I try to make filtering people a real profession.

85

My professional appearance fools a lot of people, **especially** myself.

It seems that when the filter is completed,

I can't see them as all right...

and still feel ok about. myself.

So maintaining the filter becomes a matter of survival!!

THEY ARE THE PROBLEM !

Sometimes a person talks with me about the people he filters,

and both of us build stronger filters.

At other times a person wants to talk with me about people he filters,

and he doesn't realize that our filters are different, so I filter him!

Sometimes I see a big filter
pointed at people like me,
so I escape.

When I deny myself, I help the
others build their filter

Sometimes when I feel lonely, I find someone to look through my filter with me,

I'm sure glad we aren't like that.

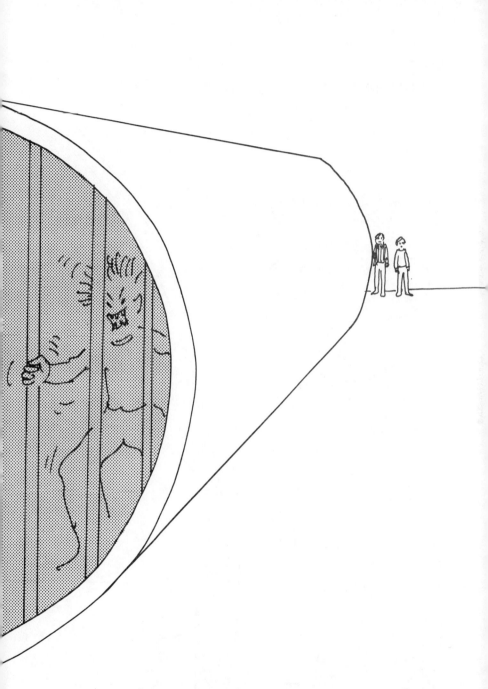

and while we are looking, my filter
grows stronger.

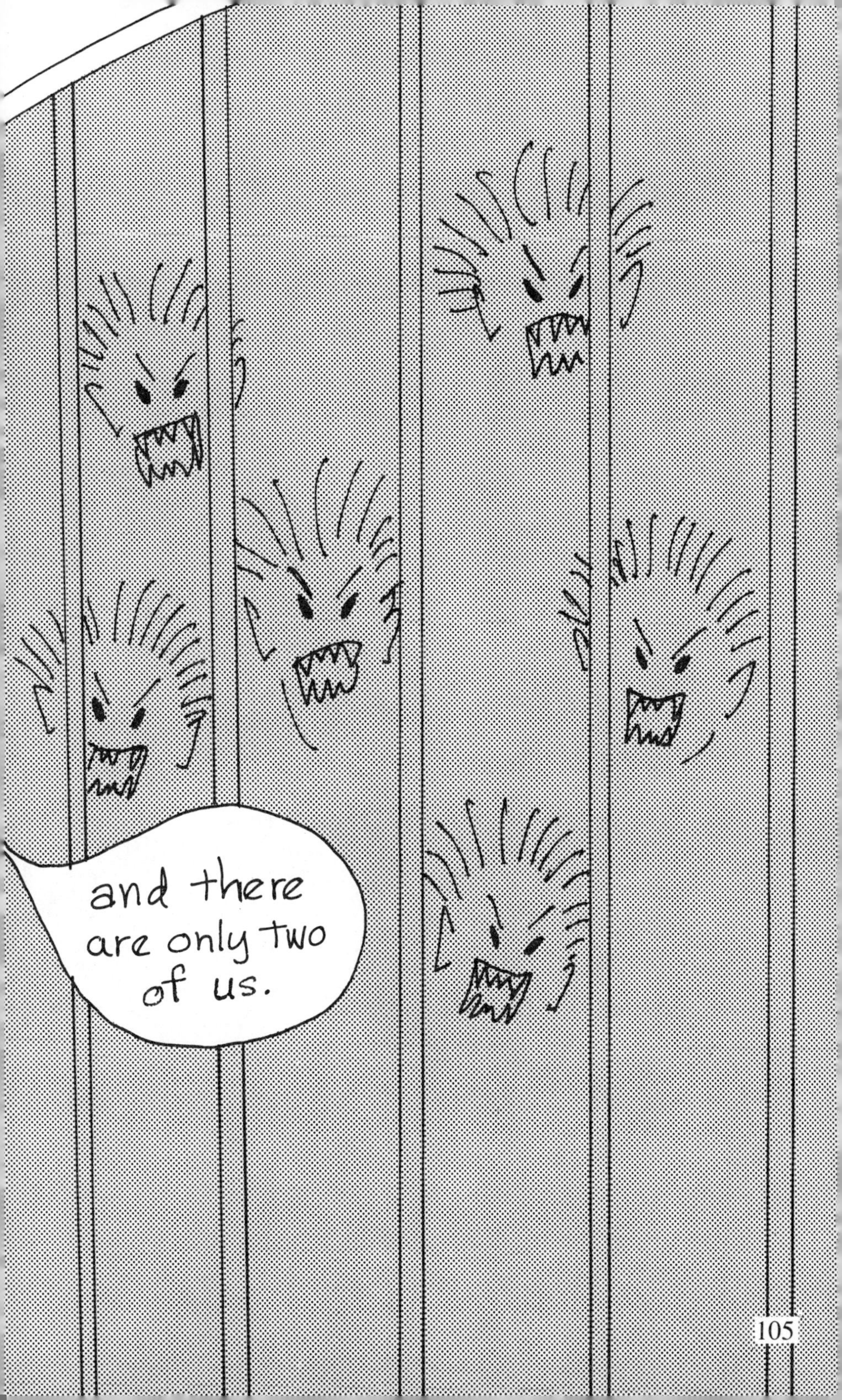
and there are only two of us.

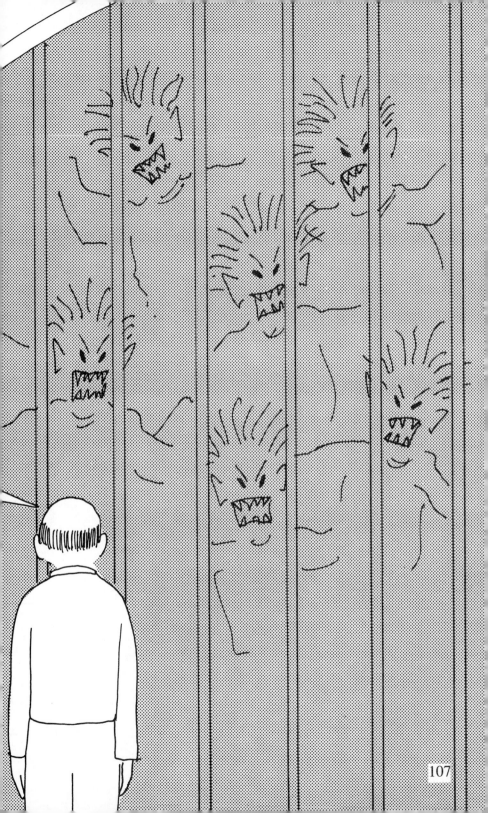

Sometimes we get so many people looking
through one filter that we don't even
know each other,

much less which people to point our filter toward.

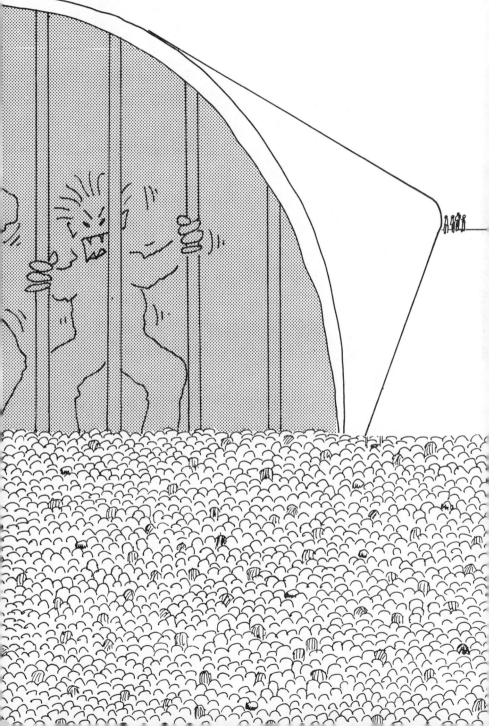

We wear signs and say special words.

111

With so many people looking through one filter, we don't even know what to see,

so we get someone to tell us what to
see and <u>we</u> believe <u>him</u>.

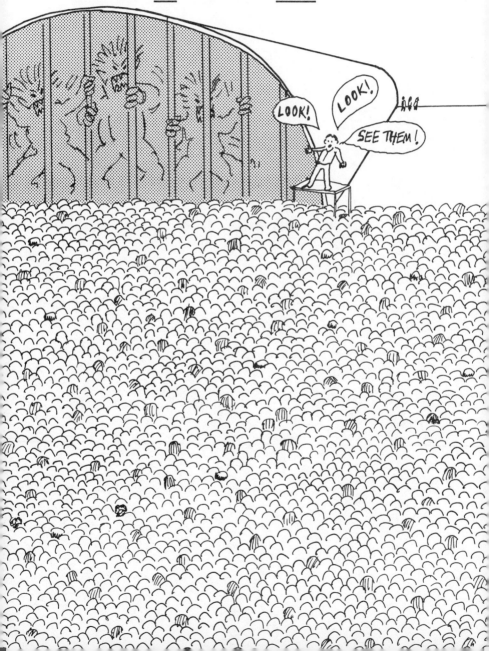

Sometimes we have more than one leader who tells us what to see,

and they tell us different things.

so we see what we fear
and become more frightened.

117

When we are frightened, we do all
sorts of things to protect ourselves
from **them** !

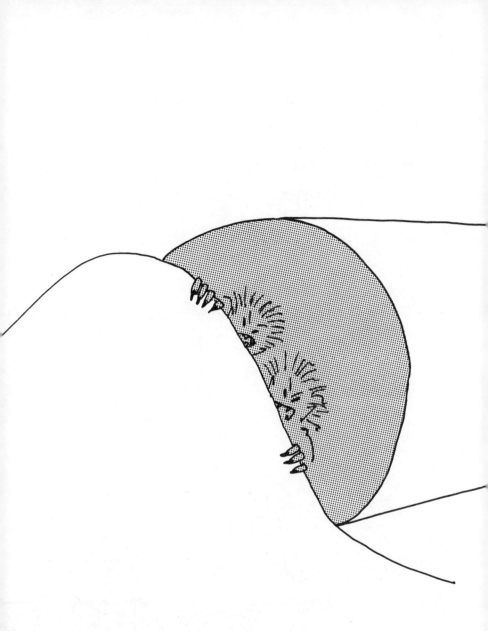

When they see us protecting
ourselves, they do more
frightening things.

When the fear and the efforts to
protect ourselves are running very
high, everyone is either looking
through our filter

or being seen through it!!

Once we are fearful and protecting
ourselves, our leader cannot easily
turn us around

because we might filter him.

When many of us learn to use filters
for protection,

we use them on each other.

because it would weaken my filter,

and the filters of those who helped
me build mine.

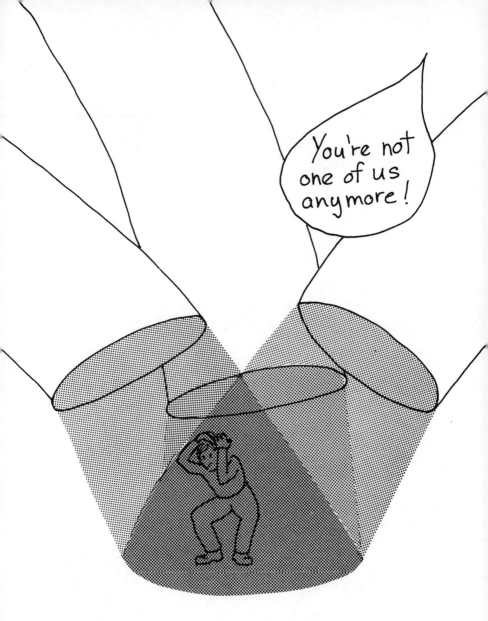

When they filter me, I feel small and weak and very alone.

So I filter them!

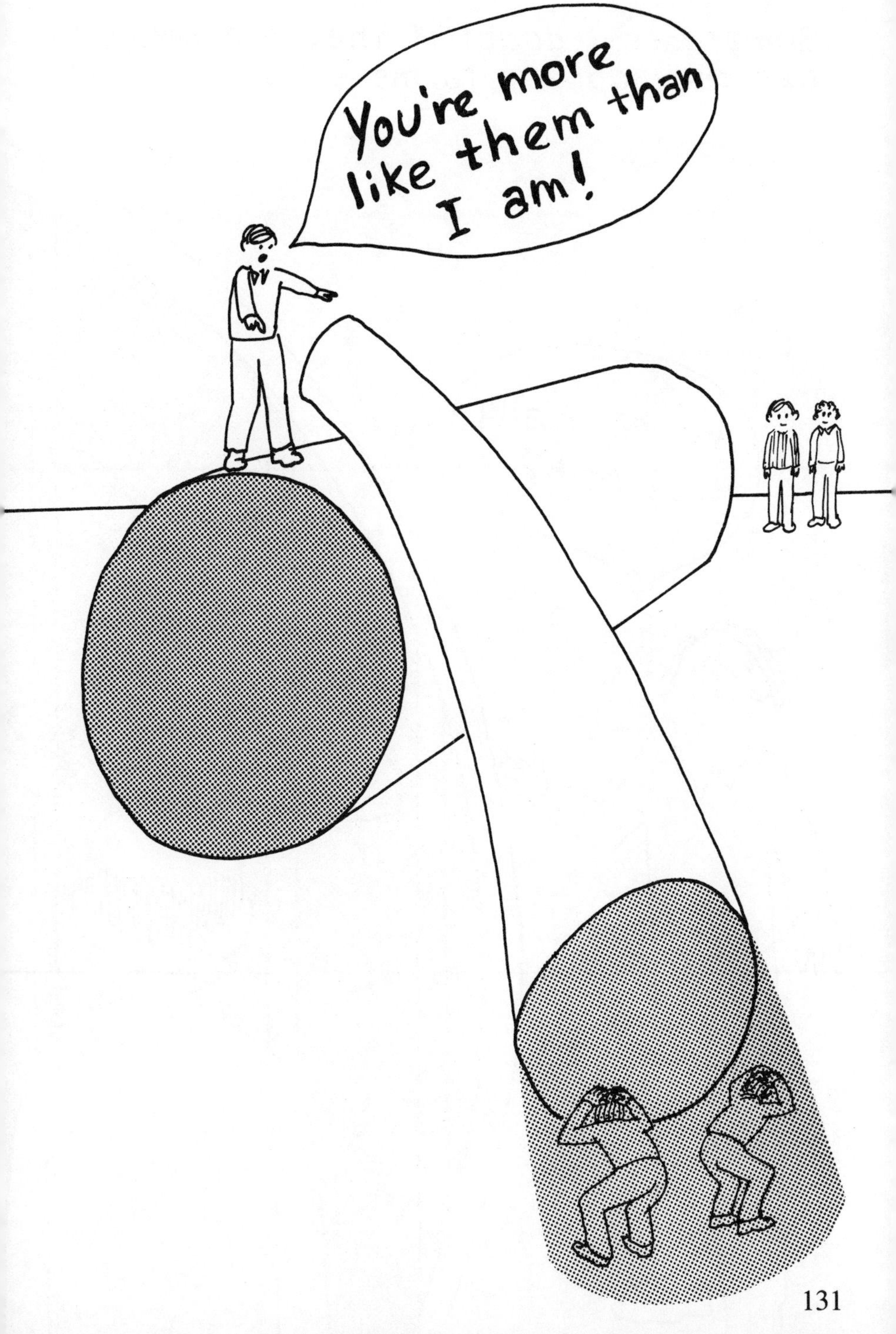

Sometimes I doubt if they are really like they appear to me.

Sometimes I just don't feel a need to filter them...

At times I doubt my filter and need to examine the situation.

Other times I doubt what I see through the filter.

So I venture off alone to know them.

But, just in case the filter is right,
I don't take any chances...

and when I do arrive to get
acquainted, they won't trust me...

and they aren't nice to me.

Then I realize...

they are filtering me.

When I'm feeling filtered, it seems that I can easily find support

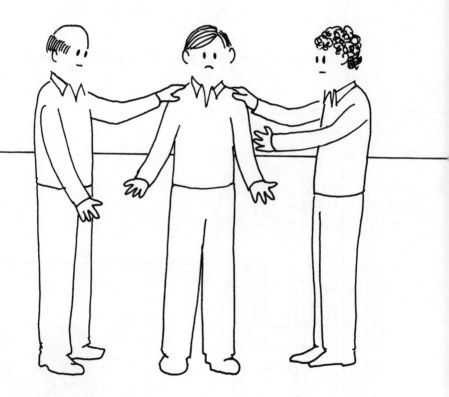

from those who look more like me.

Yet, I don't want support in ways which build more filters between myself and people who appear different from me.

When I get filtered, it hurts to feel I'm being judged

by someone who really doesn't know me.

Yet, when people do know me
they don't filter me.

Sometimes some of us want to help those who have been hurt by filters like ours.

Then we discover that they are looking at themselves through our old filter.

They are helping us get back behind
our old filter to see them.

So we devise a way of dealing with them
which we call "help".

It's a method which still protects us

from knowing them and reduces our feelings of guilt.

Yet, when I try to understand the backgrounds of these people, it really doesn't make sense to judge them.

Judging people is only easy when I don't understand.

or questioning **myself**.

It takes me a long time to realize
that I can't really learn about them
through somebody else's filter,

even when he seems to be more
experienced than I am.

When I do listen to these people and hear what has happened to them

and the situations they are in...

their behaviors make sense.

I don't need to protect myself from hearing them.

Sometimes when I really hear them
I feel guilty

for having looked at them through
my filter.

Then I understand that feeling guilty leads me back

to the filter for comfort and feelings of strength,

or it leads me to filtering others

who think the way I used to think.

So I need to accept myself and
accept what I might have done.

When I'm not looking through a filter, I don't need those

who tell me what to see.

Those who want me to see
frightening things

don't seem so *bright* or *brave.*

'Sometimes I'm a little bit lonely not being "in" on filter building.

Yet, it seems like being with other people is more meaningful

and more rewarding when I am not looking through a filter.

the more difficult it becomes for
those around me to use filters.

It's still frightening to really listen
to these people,

for to do so might change me.

Yet when I hear them... *really hear them,*

179

You mean that you were only asking... It meant something quite different to me.
It's funny I used to think you were...
they're not so likely to filter me and we listen to each other.

While we are getting to know each other,

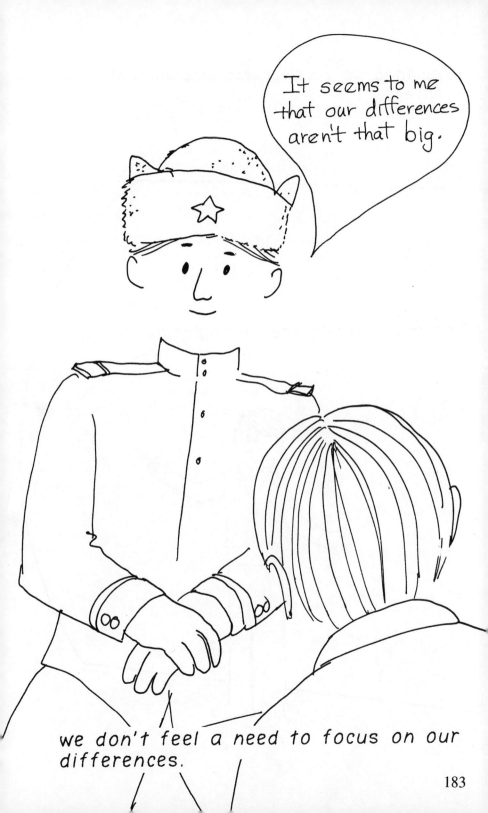

As long as I saw them through the
filter,

I really didn't see these people at all,

so understanding them was impossible.

It seems that when I doubt myself,
I feel a need to judge others.

When I accept myself, I don't need to focus on our differences with a filter.

Then it occurs to me ...

When we allow ourselves to look past our differences,

we can appreciate our similarities,

recognize our connectedness,

and enjoy the diversities that we people share.

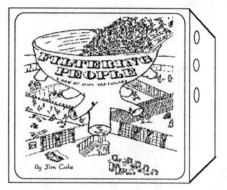
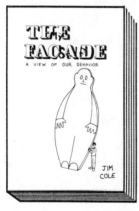
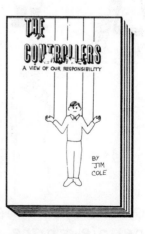

Thwarting Anger

Thwarting Anger looks into our resis-
tances to experience and express anger
and to problems related to anger. It sug-
gests ways of dealing with anger that
avoid harming others or ourselves.

A complete list of tapes and books by Jim Cole are available from:

**GROWING
IMAGES**

Publishers Services
P.O. Box 2510
Novato, California 94948

"Picture Books of the Human Experience"

"Filtering People is a gem! Its unpretentious text and simple illustrations deftly lead the reader to new insights about how we use fears and "isms" to divide us. It pricks the pompous balloons of the armchair liberal as surely as those of the archconservative. Most important, it teaches simple, personal steps that each of us can take to end bigotry."

—Paul C. Bayless, President
American Association for Affirmative Action

"Filtering People is a quick, easy-to-read, walk-through tool for holding the mirror up to ourselves to see the way in which we create images of people—images often far removed from these people as they really are. After reading Mr. Cole's insightful book, you will find yourself continually revising your first impressions of individuals and of groups. Excellent as a teaching tool as well as for personal reflection."

—Jerome B. Ernst, Executive Director
National Catholic Conference for Interracial Justice

"Filtering People is an important effort at consciousness raising. The non-threatening way it points out the absurdity and destructiveness of sexism, racism, and other types of prejudice will surely enhance the psychological health of its readers."

—Joan C. Chrisler, Ph.D., Spokesperson
Association for Women in Psychology

"People with disabilities, in most cases, would love to see an immediate change by society in prejudging their circumstances. . . . Your book creates an awareness element beneficial to all."

—Gerald Snyder, President
National Association of the Physically Handicapped, Inc.

"The effort to overcome prejudice in society is a long-term one. This book uses a creative means for focusing the attention of the reader to their own prejudices and contributes to the struggle of all minority groups."

—Jeffrey Levi, Executive Director
National Gay & Lesbian Task Force